How to Advoc [barcode: M000207614]
Food Allergic Child:

A Manual for Getting What
Your Child Needs at School

by

Laurel J. Francoeur, Esq.

Greenlaurel Solutions, LLC

4231 Lexington Ridge Drive
Lexington, MA
Email:info@greenlaureldocuments.com

Website: www.greenlaureldocuments.com

Table of Contents

About the Author

Laurel Francoeur graduated from Massachusetts Institute of Technology with a Bachelor of Science degree in Political Science and a minor in Philosophy. She is also a graduate of Suffolk Law School and has been a practicing lawyer since 1996. She is a support group leader for the Asthma and Allergy Foundation of America and served on their board of directors. She is also on the steering committee for the Food Allergy Initiative. She has appeared on ABC News talking about her experiences as a parent of a food allergic child. Laurel has also been quoted in the Boston Parents Paper. She has drafted legislation in Massachusetts which now gives students easier access to life-saving medication, and Laurel has also testified at the state and federal level about food allergy issues.

**Dedicated to my son Jeremy
for his courage and compassion**

Chapter 1 - Introduction

"Power isn't control at all — power is strength, and giving that strength to others. A leader isn't someone who forces others to make him stronger; a leader is someone willing to give his strength to others that they may have the strength to stand on their own." – Beth Revis, Across the Universe

Your child has just been diagnosed with a food allergy. Now what? Your life has changed. You cannot look at situations the same way. What used to be simple now requires lots of advance planning. You may be wondering how he will navigate during the school day with all the challenges that he will face there. You may feel powerless. Be assured that you do have the power to keep your child safe. With a few simple tools, you can help your child.

This book is designed to teach you how to advocate for your child to get the services he needs. While principles discussed here are applicable world-wide, this book focuses on solutions specific to United States federal and state laws.

This manual is unique because it provides you with a link to create your own customized form. Greenlaurel Documents has developed a software program that guides you through the form-making process by asking you simple survey-style questions. When you have completed the survey, the program will produce your customized form. This form can be saved, edited, and printed to present to the school for each year your child is in school. You can then use this form as a starting point for negotiations with your school district. Because it can be edited, you can go back to the form to make any changes suggested by the school.

The pronoun "he" is used throughout this book. This is done for convenience only, and anytime "he" is used, it should be understood that it means either "he" or "she."

The terms "parent", "guardian", and "caregiver" are similarly used interchangeably throughout this document.

Disclaimer: The content contained herein is intended for general information purposes only, and does not constitute medical or legal advice. You should not act or rely on any information without seeking the advice of a physician or an attorney.

Chapter 2 – What is an Advocate?

"I have different hats; I'm a mother, I'm a woman, I'm a human being, I'm an artist and hopefully I'm an advocate. All of those plates are things I spin all the time".- Annie Lennox

The Merriam-Webster Dictionary defines an advocate as someone who

(1) pleads the cause of another; *specifically*: one that pleads the cause of another before a tribunal or judicial court;

(2) defends or maintains a cause or proposal;

(3) supports or promotes the interests of another.

Anyone has the power to be an advocate. You can plead your child's case, and it is your job to support and promote the interests of your child. You don't need a fancy degree or influential connections. You do need confidence in yourself. As a parent, you are used to being the voice for your child. You need to take that same voice and be willing to use it in whatever context is necessary to keep your child safe and happy.

The following are the qualities you need to be a successful advocate:

1. Be Knowledgeable

A good advocate is someone who is knowledgeable and passionate about his subject. Educate yourself about food allergies in general and also the specifics about your child's allergy. The more you know, the better you can address all the needs your child will face.

2. Be Passionate Without Being Obnoxious

If you do not believe in your cause, no one else will either. Speak from the heart and let the school know why the issues are important to you. Let them know that you are afraid for your child's safety and mental well-being. However, don't go overboard and get too emotional. Do not act mad or mean – just passionate.

3. Know Your Rights

An advocate knows what rights are available and who is in charge of enforcing those rights. Read as much as you can about your rights and even consult an attorney if necessary. A summary of the most important rights is provided in Chapter 4.

4. Know the Players

Identify who at your school is responsible for overseeing your child. Learn the names of the main players like the school nurse, the principal, and the teacher. Use every opportunity available to familiarize yourself with these people so you can understand their personalities. Pay attention at parent/teacher conferences and school activities to how the players act and treat children. Ask other parents about their dealings with the school.

5. Write Everything Down and be Organized

Any time your child encounters a problem at school, make a written note about it, listing as many of the facts and circumstances as possible. Take notes when you have meetings with the teacher, nurse or principal. Make all formal requests to the school in writing. Keep copies of all reports and letters about your child. Make sure all your documents are organized so that you can find them quickly and easily when you need them.

6. Anticipate Objections

You need to be like a good chess player who can anticipate his opponent's moves. Try to think of the problem from the school's perspective. What things do you think they will find objectionable? What reasons might they give to deny your requests?

7. Offer Solutions

After you have thought about what objections the school may have, try to think of solutions that will be mutually agreeable. For example, if the school does not want to have to pay for hand wipes for the children to use after lunch, suggest that the students hand wash in the sink for free. If you cannot think of solutions on your own, ask the school personnel to help you brainstorm. Bringing a prepared form can help. In order to create the form, you have already thought about the best solutions for your child. Having the form prepared ahead of time can also help you to think about what objections the school may raise. See Chapter 6 for creating your own form.

8. Be a Teacher

Approach every interaction as if you were a teacher whose job it is to educate your child's caregivers. Good teachers are patient. You will get better results if you view your role as helping the school to learn about your child and his needs than by being a bully who demands his own way.

I want to make it clear that I am not talking about becoming a lawyer. Lawyers are special forms of advocates who receive training in the law and are able to practice law for profit in courtrooms and the like. You can be an advocate for yourself and your child without practicing law. *CAUTION: do not use your advocacy skills to advocate for someone other than your child.*

At some point, however, you may need to hire the services of a lawyer. This book is intended to teach you how to get what your child needs yourself. Sometimes, situations arise that require more expert knowledge. Never be afraid to hire a lawyer in those situations.

This manual cannot guarantee individual results. However, it can guarantee that you will learn the skills you need to help your child. Once you develop these skills, you can use them in other aspects of your child's life.

Chapter 3 – Do I Need to do Anything?

Maybe not.

Perhaps your school has a comprehensive food allergy policy that addresses all of your concerns already.

Perhaps your child's allergy is not life-threatening and/or is not very sensitive.

Some parents of food allergic children are content to send their child to school without asking for any accommodations. They think their children are mature enough to handle themselves or they may not want their child to be labeled as the "problem child." This is certainly your right. In practical experience, however, it is better to be safe than sorry. A written plan ensures that everyone in the school is on the same page and that there is no confusion about how your child's allergy should be handled. You may think that you have adequately explained your child's condition only to realize that when the time comes, your words were misunderstood or forgotten. Not all personnel may be aware of the school's allergy policy, especially when there is a substitute teacher. A reaction causes panic, and even the best educated children may not be able to handle themselves during a reaction, or may be incapacitated and not able to help themselves. It is vital that the school personnel know what to do during the crisis of a reaction – every second counts. You cannot afford to hope that they will know what to do. A written plan is the best way to ensure that the right actions will be taken. Your child's life is worth taking the time to get it right.

Chapter 4 – Know Your Rights

"People tend to forget their duties but remember their rights". -Indira Gandhi

If your child has life-threatening food allergies, he may have a disability that is recognized for special services under U.S. law.

A) Individuals with Disabilities Education Act

The Individuals with Disabilities Education Act ("IDEA") was passed in 1975. This law ensures students with disabilities a free and appropriate education. The disability must fall within one of the specific categories defined by the law. The disability must adversely affect a child's educational performance and/or ability to benefit from general education. The law provides federal funding to states and local school districts to help cover the costs of providing special education.

Students who qualify are entitled to supplemental educational services and supports to ensure that the child has access to and benefits from the general curriculum. Under IDEA, the student must have an individualized education program that specifically addresses their disability and outlines the educational services the school must deliver. In addition, a behavior intervention plan is required for any child with a disability who has a behavioral issue. Examples of related services include counseling, speech therapy, transportation, occupational and physical therapy.

In order to qualify, the student must undergo a full evaluation using a variety of assessment tools. The evaluation is meant to determine whether the child has a disability and whether the disability affects the child's education. A re-evaluation must occur every three years to determine if the services are still needed.

It is not clear whether a food allergy is a disability under the standards of IDEA. Only three cases have been decided under IDEA about a child with food allergies, and each child had other conditions as well.

B) Americans with Disabilities Act

The Americans with Disabilities Act ("ADA") was passed in 1990. It is a civil rights law for people with disabilities. Not only does the ADA apply to schools, but it also applies to private employers with 15 or more employees, all state and local government programs, and all places of public accommodation, including non-religious colleges and universities. The ADA defines a disability as "a person who has a physical or mental impairment which substantially limits one or more major life activities or has a record of such an impairment or is regarded as having such an impairment."

The ADA defines a physical or mental impairment as the following:

(A) Any physiological disorder or condition, cosmetic disfigurement, or anatomical loss affecting one or more of the following body systems: Neurological, musculoskeletal, special sense organs, respiratory (including speech organs), cardiovascular, reproductive, digestive, genitourinary, hemic and lymphatic, skin, and endocrine;

(B) Any mental or psychological disorder such as mental retardation, organic brain syndrome, emotional or mental illness, and specific learning disabilities.

(ii) The phrase *physical or mental impairment* includes, but is not limited to, such contagious and noncontagious diseases and conditions as orthopedic, visual, speech and hearing impairments, cerebral palsy, epilepsy, muscular dystrophy, multiple sclerosis, cancer, heart disease, diabetes, mental retardation, emotional illness, specific learning disabilities, HIV disease (whether symptomatic or asymptomatic), tuberculosis, drug addiction, and alcoholism[1].

The ADA defines major life activities as functions such as caring for one's self, performing manual tasks, walking, seeing, hearing, speaking, breathing, learning, and working.[2]

The ADA requires people with a disability to receive access and equal opportunity in the places where it applies. Furthermore, the ADA states that disabled individuals cannot be discriminated against on the basis of their disability. Specifically, "no qualified individual with a disability shall, by reason of such disability, be excluded from participation in or be denied the benefits of the services, programs, or activities of a public entity, or be subjected to discrimination by any such entity."[3]

C) Americans with Disabilities Act Amendments Act of 2008

Because the Supreme Court had made rulings that narrow the scope of the Americans with Disabilities Act, Congress amended the law in 2008. The amendment did not change the definition of disability, but rather stated that it should be applied more broadly. The first major change is that the amendment expanded the list of major life activities that were included in the definition of disability. Now, activities such as eating, sleeping, walking, standing, lifting, bending, reading, concentrating, thinking, and communicating are now included in the definition. In addition, the amendment broadens the interpretation of substantially limiting a major life activity. The amendment allows for impairments that are episodic or in remission to be considered in the determination when they are active. Furthermore, schools may no longer consider the impact that mitigating measures have on the definition of "substantially limits". For example, a student with food allergies cannot be denied protections simply because he has an EpiPen® that would stop an allergic reaction. The school must consider the condition without any supplemental aids.

Another change is that now public elementary and secondary schools do not have to offer Section 504 protections if a student has a "record of" or is "regarded as" disabled. The student must actually have an impairment that substantially limits a major life activity. The mere fact that a student has a "record of" or is "regarded as" disabled is insufficient.

Summary:

2008 Changes to the ADA:

-focus on including more people.

-more major life activities are included in the definition of disabled.

-conditions that are episodic or in remission must be considered when they are active.

-students must have a disability, not merely "regarded as" or have a "record of" having a disability to get services.

D) The Rehabilitation Act of 1973, Section 504

In 1973, Congress passed the Rehabilitation Act of 1973. Section 504 of that law is designed to protect the rights of individuals with disabilities in programs and activities that receive federal funds. Specifically,

> " no otherwise qualified individual with a disability in the United States... shall, solely by reason of his or her disability, be excluded from participation in, be denied the benefits of, or be subjected to discrimination under any program or activity receiving Federal financial assistance."

Section 504 uses the same definition of a disability as the ADA. However, section 504 goes further than the ADA in that it requires school districts to make special accommodations for children with disabilities. The ADA requires that disabled students be allowed into federally funded programs, but section 504 requires those programs to make modifications to accommodate the person with the disability.

However, it must be noted that section 504 does not apply to privately held institutions that do not receive federal funding, like many private schools. Although private schools may not discriminate against disabled students in the admission process, they are not required to take the extra step of making special accommodations for those disabled students. Luckily, many private schools do receive some type of federal funding, even if it's only a one-time grant. Those schools that receive any type of federal funding, even on a limited basis, must abide by section 504.

The law requires the school district to provide a *free appropriate public education* ("FAPE") to each qualified student with a disability in the school district jurisdiction. FAPE is defined as providing a regular or special education which meets the individual educational needs of handicapped persons as adequately as the needs of non-handicapped persons are met.

Child Find

School districts must actively find students who they feel may qualify for a disability. A district must identify and locate every qualified person with a disability in the district who is not receiving a free and appropriate public education. The district must also notify the persons with disabilities and their parents or guardians of their rights under section 504. This "child find requirement" only applies in grades K through 12. It does not apply to colleges or universities.

Evaluation

If the school district thinks that a student may have a disability, the school must schedule an evaluation hearing. If parents suspect that their child may have a disability, they also can request an evaluation hearing. These evaluations must occur before the school makes any placement in special education or if the school wants to make any significant change in the placement of the student.

The school must consider how the student's condition affects a major life activity, not whether the condition affects the child's ability to learn. Be aware of this – many schools try to deny students with a food allergy a 504 plan because they think the allergy does not have an impact on learning. The question is the effect of the allergy on a major life activity, not learning.

School districts must draw from a variety of sources in the evaluation process and consider all significant factors related to the student's condition. These sources and factors may include aptitude and achievement tests, teacher recommendations, physical condition, social and cultural background, and adaptive behavior. The school cannot make presumptions about the student's abilities nor can it consider stereotypes. All sources of information used by the school must be documented.[4] Under Section 504, however, the school is not required to pay for an independent evaluation of the student.

Section 504 requires "periodic" re-evaluations but does not specify a time frame. Re-evaluations every three years may be appropriate, but best practice is to conduct a re-evaluation every year.

Additionally, Section 504 requires a re-evaluation before any significant change in placement.[5]

Placement

Once it has been determined that a child qualifies for a 504 plan, the school must hold a placement meeting. Placement decisions must be made by a group of persons who are knowledgeable about the child, knowledgeable about the evaluation, and knowledgeable about placement options. School districts usually have a 504 coordinator who schedules these meetings. Typically, the 504 coordinator, the principal, the school nurse, the child's teacher, and the child's parents are present at the placement meeting.

Accommodations

Section 504 requires schools to make accommodations so that children with disabilities can participate in school activities.

The federal courts have defined an accommodation as, "generally any change in the ... environment or in the way things are customarily done that enables an individual with a disability to enjoy equal opportunities." [6] An example of a typical accommodation would be to allow the student to bring his own snack for snack time.

Reasonable Accommodations/Undue Burden Standards

Must the accommodations be reasonable? Can the school deny a request for an accommodation because it is would create an "undue burden"? According to the federal Department of Education, no. The federal Department of Education ("DOE") has said *unequivocally* that, in regard to disabled students in elementary and secondary schools, reasonableness is not the standard.[7] Therefore, the school must provide any services necessary for that student to receive FAPE. Furthermore, the DOE's position is that "neither the fundamental alteration nor undue burden defense is available in the context of a school district's obligation to provide a FAPE under the IDEA or Section 504."[8] The DOE's view is that only colleges and universities can argue that an accommodation may pose an undue burden since colleges are not required to provide a free and appropriate education.

In contrast, some federal courts have applied the concepts standards of "reasonable accommodations" and "undue burden" to elementary school education. Some judges and hearing officers at the elementary school level have used these cases to argue that accommodations must be reasonable and not impose an undue burden on the school. They have not seen the distinction between schools and colleges that the DOE recognizes. Their reasoning is based on an understanding that the ADA and Section 504 are basically to be interpreted in the same manner. [9] For example, the First Circuit Court of Appeals has found the reasonable accommodation doctrine applicable when an elementary school had to determine whether a student, because of his disability, should be exempt from a private school's disciplinary code.[10] Also, in Massachusetts, a hearing officer for the Bureau of Special Education Appeals ruled that, under a Section 504 analysis, the cost to the school for providing a peanut-free school must be taken into account when deciding if a total peanut ban would be a reasonable accommodation. In that case, the hearing officer found in favor of the ban, but she made it clear that the school could raise the defense of undue burden and that accommodations must be reasonable.[11]

So who is right? It would seem that the DOE has the federal regulations on its side. The federal regulations that specifically address nondiscrimination on the basis of handicap in programs for preschool, elementary, and secondary education do not mention any defenses available to schools – neither the reasonable accommodation nor the undue burden.[12] It seems appropriate to make the distinction between discrimination in elementary and secondary schools versus colleges and employers – after all, FAPE applies to elementary and secondary schools. Free is free, so the financial burden should not be a consideration when FAPE is involved.

Does this mean that you school may try to claim that your accommodation is unreasonable or an undue burden? Perhaps.

You can inform your school about the U.S. Department of Education's view that they should not consider what is reasonable or an undue burden, but you cannot guarantee that the school will agree or that that view will stand a legal challenge. If your school insists that your proposed accommodation is a burden, know that the school district may not "simply embrace what was most convenient for faculty and administration" but instead must consider "alternative means, their feasibility, cost and effect on the academic program."[13] Furthermore, their consideration must weigh the burden of the school with the needs of your disabled student. The needs of the other children in the school should not be considered. [14]

My best advice is to explain to the school why your accommodation is necessary to guarantee your child equal access. Take any disagreements you have with the school about any specific accommodation to the DOE or to a special education lawyer. There is no clear answer. Focus on the areas of agreement and argue about the others later.

Summary:

There is disagreement about whether an accommodation at the elementary and secondary level must be reasonable and also whether the school can argue that a certain accommodation causes an undue burden. Shift the focus to the accommodation being necessary for your child. If you get stuck on these issues with your school, seek guidance from a special education lawyer or the federal Department of Education.

Due Process

The school district must have a grievance process in place for the resolution of section 504 complaints. The district must designate a person who will coordinate the school's 504 responsibilities.

Because section 504 is a federal law, the federal government offers a means for parents to have their grievances heard. The Office for Civil Rights ("OCR") is in charge of resolving problems between school districts and parents. The OCR can also investigate a school district's denial of a 504 plan. For more information about the OCR complaint process, see Chapter 8.

Retaliation

Retaliatory acts are prohibited. A school district is prohibited from intimidating, threatening, coercing, or discriminating against any individual for the purpose of interfering with any right or privilege secured by Section 504.

Privacy

The school is not allowed to use any special codes on a student's transcript or report cards to designate the student as having a 504 plan or a disability. However, the school can mark the student's internal academic file to indicate the presence of accommodations, but the student's privacy must always be protected.

Summary:

Section 504 protects students with disabilities. The law requires schools that receive federal funds:

- To find qualified disabled students and notify them of their   rights.

-To provide disabled students with a free and appropriate public education.

- To make necessary accommodations to ensure that disabled students needs are met as adequately as the needs of non-disabled students.

-To extend accommodations to extracurricular activities and services, such as meals and recess, to the best extent possible.

-To provide a grievance procedure and a notification of rights.

E) Is a Child with a Food Allergy "Disabled"?

This is the $64,000 question. Unfortunately, each case is unique. The ADA was written broadly and therefore, does not list specific illnesses or conditions that will automatically meet the definition. The 2008 Amendments to the ADA make the determination easier, but not conclusive.

The Land Case

In 1998, the eighth district federal circuit court in Arkansas decided the case of *Land v. Baptist Medical Center*, 164 F.3d 423 (8th Cir. 1998). This case has been considered the leading case on the issue of food allergies as a disability. In *Land*, a child named Megan was allergic to peanuts. Megan broke out in hives at a daycare facility at the Baptist Medical Center. After her second allergic reaction at the daycare center, Megan was no longer allowed to enroll there. Her mother sued under the ADA, and the court found that Megan's allergy did not substantially limit her ability to eat or breathe and therefore the ADA did not apply.

The Knudson Case

Knudson v. Tiger Tots Community Child Care Center is a recent, much-publicized case from Iowa. In Knudson, a mother and father wanted to enroll their child in a daycare center. The director of Tiger Tots Community Child Care Center told the parents that because their child had a "sensitive allergy," the center would not be able to meet her special needs and refused to enroll her. The parents sued under the Iowa Civil Rights Act, which was modeled after the ADA. The lower court dismissed the case on the basis that the food allergy was not a disability, relying on the *Land* case discussed earlier in this chapter.

The parents appealed to the Iowa Appeals Court, which overturned the lower court's dismissal. The Appeals Court recognized that under the 2008 amendments to the ADA, the child's allergy falls under the category of an illness that is "episodic or in remission." However, the lower court failed to determine whether her allergy would substantially limit a major life activity when active, as the ADA requires. The case was sent back to the lower court for it to decide the issue of whether her food allergy should be considered a disability. The attorney for the plaintiff in *Knudson* describes it this way: "It would be fair to say that *Knudson* means that a child with a food allergy is no longer considered to be outside the definition of disability as a matter of law, but instead the cases must be evaluated on a case-by-case basis." What this means is that courts cannot automatically say food allergies are not a disability, but neither can they say that food allergies are always a disability. Unfortunately, many in the media and in the food allergy community have missed this point and claim that *Knudson* gives more rights than it actually does.

Lesley University Case

On December 20, 2012, the OCR heard a case against Lesley University, a private college in Cambridge,

Massachusetts. All Lesley students were required to pay for a school-sponsored meal plan. One student who had celiac disease brought a case against the university, claiming that forcing her to buy a meal plan when she could not eat many of the foods in the plan was a violation of the ADA.

The parties reached an agreement whereby the university agreed, among other things, to provide gluten-free and allergen-free food options in its dining halls and to allow students with allergies to pre-order their meals. The university also agreed to train food service personnel on food allergy-related issues, and to provide a dedicated space in the dining hall to store and prepare allergen-free foods.

The Lesley case is a huge step forward in the rights of students with food allergies. However, it is specific to the facts of the case and does NOT require all universities, schools or restaurants to make modifications to their menus for allergies. Colleges and restaurants can refuse an accommodation if it would cause a "fundamental alteration" in the service, which is a change so significant that it changes the essential nature of the services the business provides.

Hidden Disabilities

In addition, Section 504 allows for the consideration of "hidden disabilities." The OCR defines "hidden disabilities" as "physical or mental impairments that are not readily apparent to others. They include such conditions and diseases as specific learning disabilities, diabetes, epilepsy, and allergy. "[15] Please note that although the OCR gives allergies as an example of a hidden disability, this does not mean that allergies will always be recognized as a disability. Many authors have mistakenly taken this to mean that because OCR used allergies as an example, they will always be considered a disability. That is not true. As seen from the cases discussed above, the determination of a disability is based on many factors.

Conclusion

In most instances, the school district will find that a child with life-threatening food allergies does qualify for services under the ADA. However, it is important to note that the question of whether a food allergy is a disability is decided on a case-by-case basis. So far, there have been NO cases that have said a food allergy is always a disability. In fact, in December of 2012, the US Department of Justice specifically said that whether a food allergy is considered a disability depends on several factors, like the severity of the child's allergy. If you take the position that simply having a food allergy qualifies your child as disabled, you may not win. [16] A good advocate understands the subtleties of his position. Although in the majority of cases your child's food allergy will be considered a disability, be prepared to show to the district how the allergy specifically meets the definition (e.g. his allergy can cause a drop in blood pressure, thereby affecting his circulatory system). You may want to ask your child's doctor to explain in a note exactly how your child's allergy affects a "major life activity.

Summary:

The mere fact that your child has a food allergy may not be enough to show a disability. There have been no cases to date that say a food allergy automatically qualifies for protection. The position of the U.S. Department of Education is that each child must be viewed on a case-by-case basis. However, the 2008 amendments to the ADA should make it easier to show that your child is disabled.

F) Can a school claim that it just "doesn't do 504 Plans"?

Not if it receives federal funds. If your child has a disability or if the school suspects your child has a disability, they must conduct an evaluation under 504. Even if you are the only parent at your school to request it, do not let the school tell you that is not their policy. File a complaint with the U.S. Department of Education if your school refuses.

G) School Lunch

The U.S. Department of Agriculture ("USDA") has regulations[17] that require substitutions or modifications in school meals for children whose disabilities restrict their diets for schools and who participate in the National School Lunch or Breakfast Program. A child with a disability must be provided substitutions for foods when that need is supported by a statement signed by a licensed physician. For example, a disabled child with food allergies can request a school meal that is free of his allergens.

If your school is unwilling to make appropriate substitutions, you can file a complaint with the USDA, Director, Office of Civil Rights, Room 326-W, Whitten Building, 1400 Independence Avenue, SW, Washington, D.C., 20250-9410, or call 202-720-5964.

However, you cannot sue your school in state or federal court for failure to make the substitution.[18] In fact, a school district or a cafeteria worker cannot be held liable in court for damages if they accidentally feed peanut butter to a peanut-allergic child. Instead, you must file a complaint with the USDA.

H) What If My Child Does Not Have a Disability?

If your child's condition does not meet the definition of a disability, you may still be able to get your school to make accommodations. Many parents formulate an Individualized Health Care Plan ("IHCP"). For more on an IHCP, please see Chapter 6.

If you think your child meets the definition but the school disagrees, you have rights. Your school district must provide you with an impartial hearing when you disagree with their findings – even if their findings are that your child does not have a disability. School districts with 15 or more employees must have a Section 504 compliance officer and a formal grievance procedure. The details of the procedure are left to the judgment of the school district. However, the procedure must be clear and available to the parents.

You also have the option to challenge the school's denial of a disability in court, even if you choose not to follow the school's grievance procedures.

Chapter 5 – Approaching the School

"Speak softly and carry a big stick". – President Theodore Roosevelt

Your job as a parent is to get what your child needs. The best approach is to assume that you will have to educate your school district about the seriousness of your child's allergies. Show concern, but also understand the weight of the responsibility the school has.

Before you meet with school staff, you should have your pediatrician or allergist provide you with written documentation about your child's allergy. The diagnosis is crucial – without it, you have no basis for your claims that your child has special needs. Because federal law prohibits the school from getting this information, you must provide it. The more detailed the description, the better.

With the diagnosis in hand, ask to speak with the school nurse. The nurse is your most import ally. She most likely will be the one to make the determination that your child is having a reaction, and may be the person who administers the life-saving medication to your child. Because of the increased incidence of food allergy, most school nurses are aware and know how to handle a reaction. Explain to her about reactions your child has had in the past. If you know the symptoms your child typically presents during a reaction, let her know what they are. Get to know as much as you can about how she handles reactions – where she keeps the medications, who has permission to administer the medications, etc. Let her know that you are concerned about your child, but also that you respect her knowledge and you appreciate the awesome task she has in keeping your child safe. Getting the nurse on your side will make a huge difference when you get to the formal meeting. You will find that most school nurses are kind and caring people who truly want to keep your child safe. If you experience a hostile or uncooperative nurse, try to charm her. If you can't, just make sure you do not say anything that could be used against you later.

Next, meet with your child's teacher. Again, you want to show concern for your child, but show her that you respect her knowledge and you appreciate the awesome task she has in keeping your child safe. Approach her with compassion and not disdain. Ask if she has dealt with food allergies in the past and what her experience has been. Describe your child, his personality, his strengths and his weaknesses. Also, describe his history with his allergies. Ask her if she can think of creative ways to keep your child safe in the classroom. You may find that you disagree with her approach to handling allergies in the classroom. If so, do not argue with her, but save the discussion for your official meeting. You may find, though, that she has a good handle on the issues and may even be open to your suggestions. Ask what you as a parent can do, within reason, to help make her job easier. Volunteer to be the room parent, if possible. Let her know that you want to work with her, not against her.

If you have decided that your child's allergy will require special accommodations, request a meeting with your school's 504 Coordinator.

It is good practice to make this request in writing. There is no set form for this. You can draft your own request, making sure that you state that you want your child to be evaluated under Section 504. The school has a reasonable time to respond to your request.

Section 504 does not identify a specific number of days within which an initial evaluation must be completed. However it is understood that the evaluation must be conducted within a reasonable amount of time. OCR has used state timelines as a guide for "reasonable amount of time."

The school should then schedule a meeting between you and the 504 Team. Prepare yourself well for the meeting ahead of time. One of the most important things you can do is to decide on what types of accommodations your child might need. A good place to start is to draft your own accommodation plan. The process of preparing your plan will force you to think about what accommodations you will want. Having a draft plan will save you time at the meeting because you will have done the homework in advance. Sometimes schools do not like you to come with your own form; some schools have their own format. If this is the case, you can still use the form you have created as a reference for yourself to make sure that the school's form addresses everything you want. The next chapter will tell you how to draft a plan. [19]

Chapter 6 – Creating the Written Plan

There is no standardized form for making an accommodation plan. You will need to create your plan in conjunction with the school. Your written plan will contain two main elements:

1) An Allergy Action Plan which explains what steps to take when a reaction occurs

and

2) Either an Individualized Health Care Plan ("IHCP") or 504 Plan, both of which outline accommodations to help avoid a reaction.

1) **An Allergy Action Plan** is a one-page document that explains the signs and symptoms of allergic reaction and also indicates what medicine should be given to the student during a reaction. It also contains contact information so that the school knows who should be contacted in the event of emergency. Every student who has a food allergy should have an allergy action plan. Anyone in the school who is authorized to administer epinephrine should have a copy of this plan. Many schools have their own version of this form or use a premade form such as the one offered by the Food Allergy Research Education ("FARE") organization. The

allergy action plan is a distinct document, but many parents attach it to their accommodation plan.

Greenlaurel Documents has created its own version of the allergy action plan. Greenlaurel Documents has developed an interactive software program that creates the form for you. After you answer a few simple questions online, a customized form is created that you can save, edit, and reuse every year. Go to www.greenlaureldocuments.com to make your form.

The Allergy Action Plan must be signed by a physician since it authorizes the school to administer prescription medicine.

2) IHCP versus 504 Plan

You as a parent have the choice between an individualized health care plan and a 504 plan. Both documents outline the accommodations that the school must take to protect your child. However, there are significant differences between the two.

An individualized healthcare plan is a written document that explains the special medical needs of the student and what accommodations should be made to meet those needs. It is not a formal or legal document. Instead, it is usually drafted by the student's parents in conjunction with the school nurse. There is no formal grievance procedure when an IHCP is not followed.

A 504 Plan is identical to an IHCP except that it has been created within the context of the disability laws. Once agreed upon by all parties, it becomes a legal document that can be enforced if it is not followed.

Why would you choose an IHCP?

- Many parents do not like the formality of having a legal document at school. Some parents think that this creates an atmosphere of hostility between the parent and the school. An IHCP can protect your child without the rigidity of a legal document.

- Your child may be at a private school where section 504 does not apply.

- Your child may not qualify for a section 504 plan if his condition does not meet the disability definition.

Why would you choose a 504 plan?

- You create a legally binding document that has consequences if it is not followed.

- You have a means to enforce a 504 plan if it is not being followed. [20]

Both the IHCP and the 504 plan have the same basic structure. In creating either form, you must decide which accommodations are important to keep your child safe and included.

It is important that you have a good understanding of your child's allergy and the symptoms he typically presents. For example, it is important to know whether your child reacts to contact with the allergen. If so, you may want to request certain accommodations, like an allergen-free table.[21] If contact is not an issue for your child, you may not need an allergen-free table.

A good approach is to consider the various places and activities that your child will encounter throughout the school day and what issues you think your child will face. Your objective is to avoid exposure to the allergen and to allow your child to participate equally in school activities. Some of the aspects you should consider are the following:

- Classroom

- Cafeteria

- Gym

- Field trips

- Afterschool activities

- Substitute teachers

- Holidays and special events

- School bus

Your plan will contain specific instructions about the accommodations needed to keep your child safe. It is important that your plan identifies the person or persons responsible for implementing those accommodations. For example, if your child requires the lunch table to be cleaned before lunch, your plan should state that the janitor will be responsible for this task.

Summary:

You need to have a good understanding of your child's allergy and what causes a reaction. For example, does your child react to physical contact with the allergen? Take this understanding and apply it to the various situations he will encounter throughout the school day.

Use Guidelines

Many schools have food allergy guidelines or policies. The first state to develop guidelines was Massachusetts. In 2002, the Massachusetts Department of Education created an 84-page document entitled, "Managing Life Threatening Allergies at Schools." They can be found at: http://www.doe.mass.edu/cnp/allergy.pdf. Even though these are merely guidelines and are not mandatory, they offer good solutions to many dilemmas faced by food allergic students. It is a good place to start when trying to think about what your child may need at his school. The federal government is in the process of producing federal guidelines for management of food allergies in schools. These too, will not be mandatory but it is hoped that they will offer good ideas as well.

Making Your Customized Forms

Greenlaurel Documents offers you the option to make either a customized IHCP or 504 plan. When you have decided which form you would like to use, simply click on the links below for the appropriate form. These forms are interactive and do the thinking for you – you will be asked a series of questions in survey-form about possible accommodations you would like your school to consider. After you have completed the survey, your information is compiled into a form that you can save, print, edit, and use year after year. Go to www.greenlaureldocuments.com to make your form. A sample form created with Greenlaurel Document's software is included in the Appendix.

Chapter 7 – The Meeting

"When you meet someone for the first time, that's not the whole book. That's just the first page". – Brody Armstrong

If all goes well, you will arrive at the meeting with the school well-prepared. If the school has its district lawyer present at the meeting, you have the right to not participate in the meeting until you can get your own lawyer.

At the meeting, you will present your suggested accommodations to the school. This is when you will present your customized 504 Plan or IHCP form. Most likely, you will engage in negotiations with the school at this time.

The whole 504 team will be present at this meeting. It should include the principal, the district's 504 coordinator (sometimes the principal has this role), the school nurse, and the child's teacher. If you have not already received your written notice of the district's 504 procedures and your rights, you should receive it at this meeting.

Does the school have to make all the accommodations that you want? No, only those accommodations that are necessary to meet your child's needs as adequately as the needs of non-handicapped persons are met. Be prepared to show that the accommodations you request are necessary.

Section 504 does not provide schools with any federal funding. Schools, therefore, must pay for the accommodations through their general funds. However, lack of funds cannot be a reason for denying services to a qualified child. Neither can the school ask you to pay for the services. For example, the school cannot insist that you provide hand wipes for the school -the school must pay for the hand wipes.

Not all parents handle their children's food allergies in the same way. Do not allow the school to say, "Johnny's mother says he can sit anywhere and he has a peanut allergy. Why can't your child?" Every child is unique, and your child has a right to whatever protections are necessary for him. Politely remind the school of this fact and ask that discussions about other students' conditions are not only inappropriate, they are prohibited by federal privacy laws.

If your school does not have a nurse, or even if it has a part-time nurse, you should discuss at the meeting which staff members are authorized to administer epinephrine and where the epinephrine will be stored. Many states have regulations that allow a school nurse to delegate the responsibility to administer epinephrine to trained staff members. Ask who these members are and be sure that they are included in your plan. Find out if your school allows epinephrine to be stored in other places in the school besides the nurse's office. Also, ask the school when your child is allowed to self-carry and self-administer epinephrine and who makes that determination.

Many times the school will require the parent to sign a liability waiver releasing the school from liability in the event of a problem with the medication administration. This is not legal. Most states have strong "Good Samaritan" laws that protect laypeople from liability in an emergency situation. Do not sign a waiver if asked. If the school insists, then write something in the margin saying that you are signing under duress. If you are afraid to resist and sign it as is, it is likely that in the event of a lawsuit, a court would find the waiver unenforceable.

It is unlikely that you will have a final plan completed at the first meeting. You may have to meet several times before the plan is finalized.

Once the plan is in its final form, the 504 Team will sign the document. It will then be distributed to the school personnel who have a need to see it. Although you may want your child's privacy to be respected, it is best to allow many staff members have access to the form – from gym teachers to substitute teachers. That way there is no confusion among the staff about what they need to do to keep your child safe.

Meeting Checklist

- Diagnosis paperwork
- Achievement tests (if available)
- Teachers' recommendations (if available)
- IHCP or 504 Plan Form
- Allergy Action Plan
- Paper and pen/pencil
- Tape/digital recorder (if allowed)

Be prepared for the common traps:

-you do not have to pay for anything the school does.

-your child's allergy does not have to be treated like other classmates' allergies.

-you are entitled to bring a lawyer if the school brings a lawyer to the meeting. Ask that the meeting be rescheduled if you are surprised by the presence of the school's lawyer. Do not assume that you have to continue with the meeting if you want a lawyer but don't have one.

-you should be given a written copy of the school's 504 procedures, including your rights to a grievance hearing.

-do not sign a liability waiver releasing the school from liability for administering medication.

Chapter 8 – Enforcement

The best-laid plans of mice and men oft(en) go astray. – Proverb

If you have a 504 plan in place, you have legal recourse if the school fails to follow the plan. This recourse is not available, however, when the child has an IHCP.

How do I enforce a violation of a 504 Plan?

The Office for Civil Rights division of the U.S. Department of Education is responsible for enforcing the ADA and Section 504 laws. A complaint must be filed with OCR within 180 calendar days of the last act that the parent believes was discriminatory. If your case has been resolved, either by a federal, state or local court, it will not be heard by the OCR. Also, OCR does not have authority to hear cases about IDEA.

Once OCR has decided to investigate, it issues letters to both parties asking for all pertinent information. The OCR may conduct interviews and make site visits. After its review, the OCR either dismisses the case for insufficient evidence of a violation or it finds that a preponderance of the evidence supports the claim that the law has been violated. If a violation is found, the OCR sends a letter of finding to the parties. The OCR encourages the parties, however, to come to a voluntary resolution agreement and gives the parties 30 days to settle the case voluntarily. If an agreement cannot be reached, then the OCR issues a Letter of Finding of Non-Compliance. If the school still does not negotiate after a Letter of Finding of Non-Compliance, OCR will issue a Letter of Impending Enforcement Action and will again attempt to obtain voluntary compliance. If the school continues to ignore the OCR, then the OCR will either initiate administrative enforcement proceedings to suspend, terminate, or refuse to grant or continue Federal financial assistance to the recipient, or will refer the case to the Department of Justice. The OCR may also move immediately to defer any new or additional Federal financial assistance to the institution.

If a parent disagrees with the OCR's decision, he may send a written appeal with supporting documents to the Director of the Enforcement Office (Office Director) that issued the determination. In an appeal, a parent must explain why she believes the factual information was incomplete, the analysis of the facts was incorrect, and/or the appropriate legal standard was not applied, *and* how this would change the OCR's determination in the case. Failure to do so may result in the denial of the appeal. The appeal (including any supporting documentation) must be submitted within 60 days of the date of the determination letter.

Contacting the OCR

Below is the contact information for the OCR national office. Each district of the country has its own OCR

Division which will handle your case. Your local office can be found at:
http://wdcrobcolp01.ed.gov/CFAPPS/OCR/contactus.cfm

U.S. Department of Education
Office for Civil Rights
Lyndon Baines Johnson Department of
Education Bldg
400 Maryland Avenue, SW
Washington, DC 20202-1100

Telephone: 800-421-3481
FAX: 202-453-6012; TDD: 877-521-2172
Email: OCR@ed.gov

You may also be able to file a complaint in court against the school after the OCR decision. The OCR does not get involved in the court case – you must hire your own lawyer.

State Remedies

States that receive funding from IDEA must have entities like a Bureau of Special Education Appeals to allow the states to enforce IDEA. Sometimes, at the state level, you can couple a complaint involving Section 504 to a complaint under IDEA. Check with your own state about its procedures.

How do I enforce a violation of an IHCP?

There is no protocol for enforcement for an IHCP. However, that does not mean that you are without rights. The school has a duty to protect your child. In legal terms, this is known as "in loco parentis", translated, it means "in place of the parents". This is a common law doctrine that holds school staff responsible for your children while they are under the school's care. If the school is negligent in any way, you have the right to bring a case against them in court for that negligence.

You could also try to argue that the IHCP is a contract that binds the school to its obligations. This may be difficult, however, since a contract must be ratified, or signed, by both parties and both parties have to agree to be bound. Many schools prefer an IHCP for the very reason that they do NOT want to be bound.

Always start by trying to understand what happened and why things went wrong. Many times, violations are just misunderstandings or a momentary lapse. If you do not get satisfaction from the district, then you should hire a lawyer to explore your legal options.

Chapter 9 – Moving Forward

It is better to give than to receive.

You want to become known as the helpful parent at your school. It is good to take the attitude that because the school is making changes to help my son, I will do what I can to help. Volunteer every opportunity you can. Not only will you seem appreciative, you can also keep your eyes and ears on what is happening at school. For example, if you go to a Parent Teachers' Organization ("PTO") meeting, you may learn that the upcoming school fundraiser will involve selling foods with allergens, like chocolate. If you participate in the bake sale, you can see what items are offered for sale and offer to bring in something safe or ask the other parents to label foods with allergens in them.[22] Knowledge is your best ally. You need to be aware of all of the things at school that could pose a risk to your child. Also, the more the school personnel see you at school, the harder it is for them to ignore you when you need them.

Try to chaperone every event you can. I know this is a burden for working parents, but if you can arrange it, do it. You will learn from observation how the teacher deals with your child. It also can be a time to educate the teacher and other parent chaperones about the issues your child faces so they will have a better understanding and compassion for your child. For example, many times students on a field trip will eat lunch on the bus. Let the other adults and the students see what eating on the bus is like for your child – maybe he needs to wipe his hands before eating, maybe he needs to change seats so he is not next to someone eating peanut butter. People will be more receptive to learning about food allergies when they see that you are involved in the process. Perhaps they will realize that your child is not being difficult or looking for attention when he needs to make adjustments.

Reach out to other parents who have children with allergies. You can meet them at support groups throughout the country. For a list of support groups in your state, see http://www.foodallergy.org/section/support-groups. There is strength in numbers.

Offer to educate the staff and students about food allergies. Ask if you can read an age-appropriate book to your child's class about food allergies. Some examples are the Alexander the Elephant series which can be found here http://www.foodallergy.org or the No Biggie Bunch at http://www.nobiggiebunch.com. You may even want to donate one or more of these books to your school library. Make teachers and nurses aware that they can take a free on-line class called. **How to C.A.R.E.™ for Students with Food Allergies: What Educators Should Know**, offered by FARE at www.foodallergy.org.

In 2006, the federal government required all schools that received federal funds to develop a wellness policy[23]. The policy was to be designed by school personnel as well as members of the community. Find out about your district's committee and ask if you can join. This is a great way to push for food allergy-friendly policies and to learn what things your school is doing to keep its students healthy.

Get a subscription to your local paper. You need to stay on top of what events are happening in your child's school and in the district. Try to attend school committee meetings.

Does having a child with food allergies mean you have to do more work than the "average" parent? Yes. It comes with the territory when you have a child with special needs. Look at it as a blessing, not a curse. You get to spend lots of time with your child, you will have a greater understanding of your child, and you will be an integral part of your community.

Please check out www.greenlaureldocuments.com for making your own interactive form and a list of allergy-related resources.

Stay strong. You can do it. I wish you all the best so that your child will be happy and healthy.

Appendix

The following form has been generated from Greenlaurel Documents' customized software located at www.greenlaureldocuments.com. It is just an example and only contains a sample of some of the accommodations you could choose.

INDIVIDUALIZED HEALTHCARE PLAN

Student Name: Rufus Xavier Sasparilla   Birthdate: 01/01/54

Parent Name: Jane and John Sasparilla
School District: 1-239048-1239048
School: Harvard
Teacher Barack Obama
Grade: Pre-K

Beginning Date of the Plan: 09/04/12   Annual Review Date: 09/04/13

RUFUS XAVIER SASPARILLA'S KNOWN ALLERGENS:

Peanuts
Tree nuts
Soy
Milk
Shell fish
Eggs
Wheat
Fish

Does the student suffer from asthma? **Yes** *

ACCOMMODATIONS:

PARENTS' RESPONSIBILITIES:

- Parents shall provide documentation of a food allergy from a licensed provider.
- Parents shall sign consent forms to administer all medications.
- Parents shall provide a minimum of two up-to-date epinephrine auto-injectors.
- Parents shall provide the name and telephone number of Rufus Xavier Sasparilla's primary care provider and allergist.
- Parents shall provide a method to reach them should an emergency occur (e.g. cell phone, beeper, etc.).
- Parents shall sign consent forms to share medical information with the school nurse.
- Parents shall be responsible for providing classroom snacks…

SCHOOL'S RESPONSIBILITIES:

A.   GENERAL

- There shall be an Allergy Action Plan (AAP) which will be with Rufus Xavier Sasparilla at all times and appropriate adults (including substitute teachers) should have access to the AAP. The AAP should include a photo of Rufus Xavier Sasparilla, his name, specific offending allergens, warning signs of a reaction and emergency management, including medications and names of those trained to administer. The AAP should be signed by the parent and school nurse.
- The school shall train appropriate personnel in recognizing the signs and symptoms of an allergic reaction as well as the proper use of an epinephrine auto-injector.
- The school shall keep Rufus Xavier Sasparilla's medication in a safe, but unlocked place in the school, easily accessible in the case of an emergency.
- Rufus Xavier Sasparilla shall never be left alone in the event of an allergic reaction……

B.   CLASSROOM

- The school shall provide Rufus Xavier Sasparilla's classroom with easy communication with the school nurse such as classroom telephone, intercom, walkie-talkie or cell phone.
- The school shall keep Information in Rufus Xavier Sasparilla's classroom about his food allergies.
- The school shall not use food for rewards.

- If another student inadvertently brings a restricted food to the classroom, he or she will not be allowed to eat that snack in the classroom......

C.   SCHOOL LUNCH

- There shall be an allergen-only table in the school cafeteria where any student who wants to eat allergen containing foods must sit and consume them....

D.   GYM and RECESS

- Teachers and staff responsible for gym and recess should be trained by appropriate personnel to recognize and respond to exercise-induced anaphylaxis, as well as anaphylaxis caused by other allergens....

E.   SCHOOL FIELD TRIPS

- Medications and a copy of Rufus Xavier Sasparilla's health care plan must accompany him.
- A cell phone or other communication device must be available on the trip for emergency calls...

F.   SCHOOL BUS

■   The school shall prohibit eating food on school buses....

G.   BEFORE AND AFTER SCHOOL ACTIVITIES

■   A current epinephrine auto-injector shall be readily available, and an adult staff member onsite shall be trained in its use...

H.   SUBSTITUTE TEACHERS

■   The school nurse shall share and explain Rufus Xavier Sasparilla's emergency plans to the substitute teacher.
■   Any substitute teacher in Rufus Xavier Sasparilla's class must be trained in the use of an epinephrine auto-injector...

Signatures:

_____
School Representative   Date

_____
Parent   Date

_____
Parent   Date

_____
Nurse   Date

* If this were a 504 Plan, you would add a paragraph here explaining how your child's allergy qualifies as a disability – how it affects a major life activity such as breathing, eating, etc.

Endnotes

[1] 28 C.F.R. §35

[2] 28 C.F.R. §35

[3] 42 USC 12132

[4] 34 C.F.R. §104.35(c)

[5] 34 C.F.R. §104.35(d)

[6] *Thomas v. Davidson Academy*, 846 F.Supp. 611 (M.D. Tenn. 1994).

[7] See N. Royalton (OH) City Sch. Dist., 52 IDELR S 203 (OCR 2009); 20 U.S.C. § 1414(d)(1); 34 C.F.R. § 104.33.

[8] U.S. Department of Education Office for Civil Rights Dear Colleague Letter, January 25, 2013

[9] *Bercovitch v. Baldwin School, Inc.*, 133 F.3d 141 (1st Cir. 1998).

[10] Id. at 151, n. 13.

[11] Mystic Valley Regional Charter School, BSEA # 03-3629 (Massachusetts, March 19, 2004).

[12] 45 C.F.R. §84.31 et seq.

[13] *Wynne v. Tufts University School of Medicine*, 932, F.2d 19,26 and 28 (1st Cir. 1991)

[14] Mystic Valley Regional Charter School, BSEA # 03-3629 (Massachusetts, March 19, 2004)

[15] www2.ed.gov/about/offices/list/ocr/docs/hq5269.html

[16] From the Office for Civil Rights Frequently Asked Questions About Section 504 and the Education of Children with Disabilities :**"Does a medical diagnosis of an illness automatically mean a student can receive services under Section 504?** No. A medical diagnosis of an illness does not automatically mean a student can receive services under Section 504. The illness must cause a substantial limitation on the student's ability to learn or another major life activity. For example, a student who has a physical or mental impairment would not be considered a student in need of services under Section 504 if the impairment does not in any way limit the student's ability to learn or other major life activity, or only results in some minor limitation in that regard." http://www2.ed.gov/about/offices/list/ocr/504faq.html

[17] 7 CFR Part 15b

[18] *Pace v. State*, Court of Special Appeals in Maryland, September 29, 2010; *Great Lakes Consortium v. Michigan*, 480 F.Supp. 2d 977 (W.D.Mich. 2007).

[19] Even if you think the school has a good handle on allergies, it is always good to have a plan in writing.

[20] In 2005, 1.2% of K-12 students nationally were on 504 plans, with middle and high school in greater percentage than elementary school. *Section 504 and Public schools: A National*

Survey Concerning "Section 504-Only" Students, Rachel A. Holler and Perry A. Zirkel, NASSP Bulletin, Vol. 92, No.1, March 2008.

[21] The food allergy community is divided over the proper name for the table where a food allergic child sits. Many use the older language of peanut-free or allergen-free, which means that peanuts and/or other allergens will not be allowed at the table. There is a movement to change this to peanut-friendly or allergen-friendly table. Some feel the word 'friendly" is a better description because no one can guarantee 100% compliance. Also, some schools think there is less liability if they promise a friendly table rather than a free table. Use whatever language you and your school feel is appropriate.

[22] Note from author: When my son was in elementary school, it was mandatory for all children to attend the bake sale to show school spirit. The principal would announce on the loudspeaker when it was time for each class to go to buy their treats. If a child did not have money, a teacher would give him a quarter to buy something. I made sure that I was at the bake sale table whenever my son's class went to the sale.

[23] Public Law 108-265, Section 201 for participants in the National School Lunch Program.

Made in the USA
Charleston, SC
16 April 2013